D0591591

The
Island

The Island

poems by Michael White

Copper Canyon Press / Port Townsend / 1992

Publication of this book is supported by a special grant from the National Endowment for the Arts. Copper Canyon Press receives financial support from the Washington State Arts Commission and is in residence with Centrum at Fort Worden State Park.

Library of Congress Cataloging-in Publication Data
White, Michael, 1956–
    The island / Michael White.
        p.   cm.
    ISBN 1-55659-050-4 : $10.00
    I. Title.
PS3573.H4744I84   1992
811'.54—dc20   92-20136

COPPER CANYON PRESS
Post Office Box 271, Port Townsend, Washington 98368

Acknowledgments are gratefully made to the following magazines, in which versions of these poems first appeared:

The Antioch Review: "Near Light"(1)
The Cornfield Review: "The Haven"
Ellipsis: "Underway"
The Gettysburg Review: "Flight: Homage to Vladimir Nabokov"
The Journal: "Recurrence"; "The View"
The Missouri Review: "The Dream"; "Fish Creek Falls"; "The *Narcissus* Moored"; "Near Light"(3); "The River"; "The Story"
The Mississippi Review: "Elegy for Tom McAfee"
The New England Review: "The Island"
Western Humanities Review: "The Bridge" (later reprinted in New Voices: College Prize Anthology #7); "The Solving Memory of Things"
Several of these poems appeared in *This Water*, a chapbook from Silverfish Review Press.

The author would also like to thank Mark Strand, Rod Santos, Larry Levis, and Brooke Hopkins, for support which has been indispensable to his work.

This book is dedicated

to my wife

Jackie G. White

(1947 – 1991)

_____

"If it were possible to look into the sea as into glass. . . . "

—WALLACE STEVENS

CONTENTS

SOLACE

ODES AND STORIES

THIS WATER

Solace

RECURRENCE

Darkness, but
a mountain wind howled through the canyons,
through the dark-red willows bent wildly about
along the snowy banks – whining and drowning out
the sound of rapids hurtling, gnawing away at rock
and root, and the sounds the spruce made creaking: strokes
of cadmium blue on white. And somehow what
occurred to me, as it flew above
the phosphorous light-gray foothills at the ends
of streets, was a page of newsprint rising suspended
over the rooflines – flown on the gusts that dragged me from
a vivid sleep, absently stripping a frond
of the window fern in my hands. And the smoke-fog
was flushed from the back streets where it lurked
all winter, as a last haze of leaves flocked
suddenly up from the skeleton poplar,
and that hollow wailing honed against the edge
of things, against the parked cars
filmed with salt, and the darkened houses.

Already then, the white-gold skies of
January seemed an hallucination;
but spring was still holding off, and the air
was so thickly wound with dust that children might not
have known their own front lawns (such as lawns were)

if they hadn't left wagons or robots out
in random, upflung attitudes of exultation.

This scene coalesced in a minute or two,
as a window somewhere upstairs shook hard
in flurries, until I remembered your voice
on the phone: its emptiness, its limp indifference to
the crushing words you whispered.
                                    (All night I dreamt
of a river swept with gestures of mist,
with shadowy overhanging branches mirrored in it, blurred
a little in the barest riffles swirled
downstream like a tremor across a face. Nothing was sure
in that slow body of sky-filled current,
not the sound of your voice in the silence, or
the wavery shapes of trees on the opposite shore,
not even the opposite shore.)

And *that* was an ordinary day at last. The heavy light
in half-mile splashes let through gaps
in the Wasatch, fell through the ghost-gray aspen,
caught on the first of the gray-green roofs, as if
all that could happen here had happened.
And before I left, the sky made up its mind
abruptly, shearing open over the sandblown reaches
I would drive that day, where mesas and sandstone reefs

rose at me like a storm at sea that crests
beneath the weight of wind.

And suddenly, the steel-bright air
was locked in its late thaw, and everything thin —
lamp posts, flagpoles, spires of pine —
dissolved like salt in the chill March glare.
Waves of rust and amethyst throbbed up
the broken sky. How could I understand
that nothing can save you? Soon
the deep-bass Catholic bells downtown would blend
with the lisp of traffic, and crocuses would bloom,
next week, across the faded neighborhood
like a shot of clear snow water,
but I couldn't think, as panic loomed,
of that white hush, of what could hide
so long, love, in the blood.

THE VIEW

for a childhood friend

This was the edge-world overlooming the endless
Missouri floodplain. We'd pedaled the river road
The length of the county, past the sprawl of mud flats
And singed-bronze fields that flowed like a separate stream
Between the ragged lines of the limestone bluffs,
And the great meanders, lit with sun. . . .
                                        And we'd found
An old Case tractor, nearly invisible
In the dark explosion of undergrowth along
The shore, sunk to its axles in the silt,
Rusted out and draped with grapevines and leaf-drift.
We cleared the vines, tried the gears, gawked
Awhile, and left. . . .
                        Hawks were shooting the updrafts,
Skimming the blank face of the river. Winter
Was lurking like smoke around each upstream bend.
Gold of the cottonwood leaves. Flurries of locusts
Chirred up at once at the sound of our spinning wheels. . . .

                        *

We were pushing our bikes up a spur road choked with sumac,
With full-grown trunks between the tracks — a path
That was hardly more than a faint, unnaturally straight
Breach in the old-growth shagbark woods. Dust-devils
Made of leaves and wisps of mulch light whirled
Through chinks in the understory. We had to decide
To camp on that rocky, unlikely height, or head
For home, but the view, or something in the air —

A faded, vaguely rotten sweetness – stopped us.
Beyond, just over the crest, the ridge shelved out
In a stark overhang; stunted cedars
Clung on the very edge, bent back in the root
From the years of wind. A flock of sparrows was riding
Those limbs, ruffed up. As we turned back, steering the bikes
Down the rain-rutted path again, the glare
Off an angle of rusting galvanized farmhouse roof
Drew *your* eye to it, and into the orchard beyond:
The Schwinns were dead weight then, and we let them drop.

*

Some of the lower limbs were half submerged
In the tide of grass, some were broken outright
Under the weight of rose-pink Jonathans:
Our luck was changing. There were apples *everywhere*
With only the deer to eat them – so we ate
Our way from tree to tree on the deer trails winding
Through them, as a flickering rain of small white moths
Rose up from the wildly overgrown meadow,
Flooding the cider-sweet slopes of light.

*

You could see the heat waves shimmering off the roof
Plainer than you could the house itself,
Loosely clasped in a small, isolate grove
Of mountain ash that had grown up in its shade;

The blood-orange leaves wove flamelike over the weathered
And stove-in siding. It was almost completely
Blent with the view — only the chimney stood
Above. We kicked our way through the briars that closed the
      doorway,
Into the acrid dark, staggering
Across the rotted floor, instinctively stooped
And groping for walls that were sunk out of kilter. . . .

If it weren't for the chimney, the house couldn't stand,
But I couldn't see how that chimney could stand.
It was made of some poor, chalky brick the wind
Had sluiced through along every seam, leaving
Eerie, irregular, smooth-hollowed gaps
Which rayed the room with sunlight. Looking out
Through the lacy and light-riddled masonry
Was a little like staring up through leaves at fragments
Of empty sky. And that was the afternoon.
The walls were printed through with point-blank blasts
Of birdshot. None of this needed to be explained.
We were fifteen. We knew the Indian summer
Was over. Your mother was dying, wandering lost
In her labyrinth of psalms. The first real snow
Would crush that house forever into the hillside.

A moment later, an indigo dusk washed over
The ridge, and then full dark weighed down around us.
Hundreds of fireflies hemmed the orchard air.

And we just stared at the fire: when it bit a vein
Of sap, a sputtering column of sparks flew upward,
Dousing itself in the sky. When it looked burned out,
A puff of breath could rekindle the light green flames.
And without warning, an enormous halfmoon glowered
Through the doorway, and every sound of the world
Below came up to us. . . . Beyond the octaves
Of crickets, the river's rushing noise of wind
Was caught in the windless trees. Mice roamed the rafters.
I sometimes thought I could hear the ghostly wingbeat
Of an owl in full flight swooping by, but I knew
In real life, no one could hear them; I *knew* it was only
The fire flaring up, or a gust of breeze
In the flutelike chimney, or the first part of a dream,
I thought, arriving before I could sleep.

                    *

And then, sometime late, I awoke, and rose in a kind
Of slow and clumsy stupor. I couldn't see
The warped and fire-warmed floorboards underfoot,
And the place had got so wind-loose and rackety,
That what light there was—pale strokes of moonlight sieved
Through knots and nailholes in the siding—*shifted*
Slightly with each step, skewed back and forth
So much I felt like a fish, or a ghost, or a drunk.
I moved through a darkness more pronounced for the weird light

Needled into it, through a doorless door
To the last room at the far end of the house,
Which could only have been the bedroom (it was littered then
With twelve-gauge casings, and leaves, and lengths of stovepipe),
Where I let a long, luxurious stream of piss
Splash down through the broken window sashes, into
The heavy, bowed weeds below.

                And I hardly noticed
That moment of orchard framed beneath the pointed
Southern night—the luminous apple trees,
The starlit grass, the silent hornets' nests
That were clustered beneath the eaves,
                      but no one knows
What shall be given to memory. Sheer banks
Of cloudlight and starlight interwound
Like isthmus and inlet, bodies of land and sea.

And no one can know what brief, lit scenes the mind
Sets for itself.
            Worming across the vast
And lightless plain to the west, the river's course
Appeared and reappeared, rolling its
Dark silver sheets of moonlight through the trees,
Through miles of unbroken silence, heart
Of levee and hedgerow, where the tractor we found
Was lost in a fabulous tangle of undergrowth. . . .

I wondered how it got left there, thought of the farmer
Cursing wildly, watching his wheels spin free
In the muck, and finally giving up, slogging on foot
Toward home, his fields gone under the flood.

                    *

Flanking the riverlands, the soft, gray hills
Retreated north as far as I could see,
Into the soft, slow haze on the horizon,
Where a pale orange, undulant glare was smeared like blood
Across the humid air. . . .
                              It took me a minute
To recognize the gathered lights of the town
Where I lived. It was something like glimpsing your own figure
Caught in a pane of glass on the street – that lapse
Before you know yourself. But *those* were the lights
Of our parents, lights I bicycled through for years
As my father slept, lights flooding the rivery streets
And lofting a pale, discarnate glow between
The black, full-summer shapes of the oaks on the backs
Of hills, and that scattered show of clouds above them –
There it flared, like a huge, auroral scream.

                    *

What's merciful is knowing where you are.
Perhaps because my eyes were used to the darkness,
Or because a lilac-gray streak had appeared
At the base of the night-blue firmament, the house

Seemed suddenly very small. *Hours* must have passed.
I could tell which boards to walk on not to wake you.
In the living room, the fire was ash. Your face
Was cradled in one arm, and your mouth was gaping,
Unnaturally distorted by the light
Or the weight of sleep. A fine sweat shone on you.
I remember carefully shading my eyes from the sun;
I knew it would soon slip out from the edge of the world,
And I wanted to be asleep when it did. But the dawn,
In my imagining, went on unfolding
In slow, dishevelled sequences of cloudscapes
And treescapes, with tongues of sunlight swirling over
The forest floor — as if searching for traces
Of summer — and a solemn ground fog avalanching
Beneath the apple trees. . . .

       What happened next
Was nothing, but I took it as a sign
Of luck when you turned a little in your sleep,
The breath whistling in and out your lungs,
And shivered, and became yourself again.

POSTCARD

All the west
Lay clear and luminous, blue

And purple and pure dark crimson,
And then it rained like a soft shadow

Into the trees. If I could tell you
Anything, it would be how the rivers

Of aspen lining the northern ravines
Of Grandeur Peak, just turning then,

And far more gold than their riffling leaves
Could hold, were spilling them upwards, into

The air, like bright arpeggios;
How the switchbacks coiled down through

Those caverns of flames of the incandescent
Maples and oaks that live up there;

And how – if I had looked – the city
Beneath, beyond the canyon mouth,

Shook out its tentacles of lights.
If you see this, love, imagine my descent

Through waves of enormous color, the ache
In my legs which vanished with the hour

In a dreamlike glaze of orange light,
And picture me floating down through the fires

Of this day and the next.

NEAR LIGHT

[1]

Streaming winds, winds of winter pine
And the north sky's seven stars shook the glass —
And as the first clear shade of vine splayed
Inward, she lay gloved in dream,

Sifting, like a banked fire, her watery syllables —
How softly, softly. When a great cloud at sea frays,
Writhing in a mouthful of salt air,
So the lines I held, I heard —

And again the dying friend was mine,
His mind as ruined as his lungs, and not long left,
Encircled by a tone as light as flame,
Each word a lifetime, a beginning —

[2]

October slips from the coast like breath
In the wake of your body, and far along
This level sand, a fishing boat —
Upturned, rain-black — steams in the sun.

And a salt mist builds in the eucalyptus,
Welling through their sea-locked silence,
Just as an inward wound bleeds on —
As in the bay, great floats of eelgrass

Face the tide. How can it crave such solace —
Unmemoried love — in color only, drawn
From cerulean, rain-ceased air, in deeps
Now pierced, now drenched with blue?

[3]

The late warm rains have beaded the eaves and gone,
And the smoke-heavy currents of moonlight
Flooding the foothills, and the dust of long drought
Drifting minute by minute inland —

But what sun moves through the soundless street —
Through the border of plum trees — moves exhausted and common.
In my front window, half in shade,
A woman wrapped in a loose robe steps into sight,

Into the slow ambiguous shadings of her lawn;
In the upper air of my heart, a tower ascends
Through a cloudbank, like this city. But a cold lake wind
Soon changes tower, cloud, and woman into dawn.

Stories
and Odes

FLIGHT:

HOMAGE TO VLADIMIR NABOKOV

Down from the mountains, down from Catherine's Pass,
    Cloud shadows, rolling transparencies, flowed over
        The glacier lakes; and the wind raked the granite upthrusts,
Shivered the backs of the sunshot lupine meadows,
    Shivered the paintbrush and penstemon lighting
        The boulder fields, and then came apart
In a flurry of eddies among the spruce trees, folding

Its flashing folds around his shoulders as he worked
    His way downcountry, nothing but air in his net.
        Who could be so alone? Oblivious to
The swarms of purplish-brown hawkmoths which rose
    As one, and settled slowly down as one
        After he passed, the last, or next to last,
Swallowtail of 1943

Was all he thought of. So he followed it through wet
    And waisthigh grass, as he had in the Urals and Alps,
        Through a susurrous willow bog which clung and sighed
At every step, and trailed slow-filling footprints
    Behind him. And ahead? Those arabesques
        He coveted, those lemon and matte-black wings
He knew in their subtlest markings, had drifted away

In zigzags traced through the pointilistic aspen –
    Blent with the languid sunrays fanned down through
        High gaps in the leaves like the long light of his childhood,
His vanished Vyra estate . . . gutted by memory,

Wavering like a flame, its carriage road
    And arches and attics and porticoes all raveled
Piecemeal into this fir grove, and that one:

And like most of his empires and emigre haunts, it was lost
    In the wake of his long-drawn, last-ditch flight to the West;
        But there is no escape for the eye. Massing beneath him,
A hazy, burnt-gold Claude Lorrain cloud
    Suffused the canyon as if with its own light;
        And, somewhere under the dark blue apse that domed
Amphitheatric Albion Basin, the rare

"Nabokov's Pug" still fluttered maddeningly
    At large, unreal for a few more days. Each summer,
        The inked-in itineraries crossed and crosshatched,
So even the names of the scenic routes were blurred
    Together, like a terra incognita
        Of our suburbs, our mauve vistas and attendant
"Alpine Haven" or "Placid View" motels—

Which only he could invent, accustomed more
    To some vast, autumnal *Hotel du Palais*
        Which, shadowed in a throng of white resorts
Along the *plage*, still kept perpetual dusk,
    A dreary marble and mahogany
        Nineteenth-century silence, where *objets-d'art*
Lurked in the dregs of the off-season sun,

And the clear ring of a crystal pendant drilled
　　Him from a revery: who *else* should describe
　　　　Our motels? Nabokov, I imagine you
At your fiftieth, with your antique Russian valise,
　　Your baroquely-carved chess set (difficult lines
　　　　Of play start flickering through you when you touch it). . . .
Plastered with bugs, your car still ticks with heat

In the evening light of 1943.
　　For hours, you had driven east through sheets of rain,
　　　　And now you still stare out through a towering storm
In platinum gray relief, where a few low stars —
　　Wind-sharpened, solemn — swim in the nebulae
　　　　Above a sculptured stone and piñon waste.
The room is warm. You gaze out, growing sleepy,

As your shadow-brother, Sergey, might have gazed —
　　As if listening intently into the huge night falling
　　　　Upon him, driving everything that could move
Beneath the freeze. Unspeakably starved, *he* looked
　　At the fringe of spangled treelimbs over the wire
　　　　Of the German camp, and knew he wouldn't last.
As a film trails off, counts back its last scratched sepia

Frames before it draws a blank, the rainfall,
　　Having broken the back of a leonine summer,
　　　　Turns to torrents of snow. It streams through the lamplit
Nimbus floating above the huddled car-shapes;

And, as if lost in thought in a world of moths –
        In their slanting drift – the room seems to be rising
Upward slowly, like a balloon. I think

Anything might occur to you then, as against
        The desert winter, the fields of snow which promise
            To last forever, a ghostly conspiracy
Kicks up in you like an insubstantial ruin
        Of light, a Rouen Cathedral rising in fretwork
            Chords of rose and lilac: your poem *Lolita*
Burning away all night, all your life, like a wound.

THE *NARCISSUS* MOORED

after Conrad

Coming home under a light helm,
With all sails full of a cold and steady breeze,
We first took in the flying jib, then climbed
Aloft – though scarcely conscious of moving at all –
And closely reefed the stunsails and topgallants
As the river's sea reach narrowed, and the land
Slipped in between the ship and open sea.
White gulls dove down through the stripped yards.
What's left to tell? From across the bay, we could hear
The windborne racket of town, as the tugs drew near,

Streaming smoke, and slowly towed us landward. . . .
Where none could have known a passage of such calms
And headwinds, such high-running seas:
Like a dream of weeks, when combers were breaching the decks,
And below, ahead of the mast, we rolled side to side in our sleep,
As if held in the hull's echoing voice itself. . . .
Until clear waters compassed the bow, and the sails
Hung lifeless, weighted as our minds were weighted
With deafening absence, nothingness,
The sound of our own blood pounding. But aboard,

I could never quite remember her slim, high lines,
The old style stern and raking stem, all weathered
A brilliant black from the glassy sea ways –
Not as she looked amidst the clutter of that quay.
From far away, I watched the crew spill quickly out
On the stones of the Tower Hill, scattering

In rough knots as the streets rose underfoot
And they turned toward the city. I never
Saw them again. In the early thaw, I bought
A rock-built farmhouse going to seed some miles

From sight of the Pentland Firth, and let it go.
And, since this land lies deep in the lee
Of a treeless, steeply-arched hill, the moonlight
Falls here last. One night, the flutelike cry
Of some hunting bird — I wouldn't know what —
Or a shutter loose in a small land wind, woke me.
But when I turned out, there was only hearthsmoke
Floating in a webbed light on the floor,
And a dove-colored stillness over the downs, and a faint path
Threading its way through last year's grass to sea.

THE ISLAND

After a week of running before a norther,
Flying with full canvas over a violet sea,
We lost our stern wind off a strange isle's shore,
Furled sail, and leveled oars to the limpid water.

It was a steep woodland isle, hilly and long,
Dark with alder, black poplar, and wild olive,
And the salt air was smoothed with cypress and laurel;
Over the forest slopes falcons hovered and dove,
While gulls and golden cormorants floated across the shore light.

When we pulled toward the deep craggy seacliffs,
Our bow watch warned of rockfallen reefs
Beneath the still surface. . . . Dead as the wind
On the water – for hours, no one wet an oar tip –
We brought up wine and the hard loaves from below.

We thought of our headlong flight on the north wind –
As if a celestial longing had bellied the sail –
Our keel skating over the high gray swells,
And leaving a foaming sea-track to an island
Lost on a desolate, uncrossed sea of light.

But as we studied the island, a distant storm cloud
Rose low on our wake's horizon – rolling and blue –

And then the thunder clapped like an oak trunk splintering. . . .
We took our thwarts and rowed, skirting the reefs.

Not one breach in the sheer rock face, no bay nor breakwater;
No stretch of level sand, nor river mouth:
Only the cliffs, twice the height of our mast; and the unapproachable
        wall
Of trees above; with ivy everywhere, the color of wine.

Then we thought we saw a far off smoke-drift. . . .
And, between a stand of oaks and a towering promontory,
We thought something shone, like slow-moving wool.

And as we rowed, it came to seem that these islanders
Must be, by some god, held dear: for why else hide,
From the long ships, from war- and sea-scarred men,
In a wild sea's midst, and ringed with subtle reefs
And cliffs, this sweet air, this rose and emerald
And velvet black, vine-woven gloom?

A people like no other, then. Moving through
Twilight where love is common as light, at will
From shore to shore, from shadow to violet shadow,
And lying down together, too, in the early dusk,
In the mint-scented, secret mingling of shade.

And we remembered our steady flight before the north wind:
As though a celestial longing bent our mast,

Our hull shearing through the heavy wave crests,
Spreading a foaming sea track to an island
Lost on a cloudy, uncrossed sea of light.

The gathering squall darkened and woke the sea
To an endless rocking and shuddering, and the ground swells
Lapped the cliffside (the sound, after so much stillness,
Was the sound of slapped flesh) and the lowering sky
Rumbled and flashed over the blue-black waves.

In the old rhythm, we bent over our benches,
But still saw neither fire nor safe landfall –
Only the cliffs, the wind-tossed chaos of green leaves. . . .
And I imagined men watching us through the leaves,
And not only us, but staring long at the sea,
Staring long and quietly as a harborless sea
Drinks light – staring through the treelimbs of childhood,
Until strange, staggering shapes come vaguely toward them,
Until the silent, intricate burning, and the cold,
Rancorous ash of fear that is life
Must be voiced. . . . and until this day
When over the tranquil sea sails our black ship.

We'd been at sea a long time. We were burned;
Salt-streaked; our hair matted down; and our eyes
Were nearly gone from the glittering unendurable
Sun on water, sun on armor, and the nights

Of winter moon, of stars unseen on the continents. . . .
One of the men had dreamed of a place half-drowned
With rage, he said, and swore this was it. And no one spoke,
But we thought of our headlong flight before the north wind —
As if a visitant power had swelled our canvas,
Our keel plunging through the huge whitecaps,
Leaving a foaming sea track to this island
Lost on a desolate, uncrossed sea of light.

Now in darkness we traced our wide circle:
To the right, the looming cliffs and the thunderous surf;
To the left, and above and close upon us, billows
Of pale fire awash in the rising gale.
We were afraid for the slender hull in those reefs,
But we also feared the entangled will of the islanders. . . .

Shock after shock drove us drifting shoreward;
We pulled through a chill wind full of lightning and salt;
We pulled as if to break the oar hafts in their locks,
As if to tear our shoulders from our hearts.
And the island slowly wheeled away — its bone-white
Breakers and thrashing treeline sank sternward
As the gale swept us, listing, to open sea —
It whistled through the ropes and the naked mast

As if in the live fir tree.

                It blew fiercely,

And, for a moment, as the island drifted off,

I thought the isle was the wind's throat—and that the wind

Rose from its stream-cut caverns, and seethed

Through the hidden creekbeds, the withering cypress groves,

And then slashed out over the black water toward us,

Lashing the sea and the ship's ribs into the sea,

                          and then,

Though I searched intently over the pitching stern deck,

And stroke after stroke of blue-white lightning fell

The fathomless depth of the sky, the island was gone.

Now the men were leaving their worn thwarts for below,

Leaving their race for the hold's brine-bitter darkness,

Huddled in their sea-cloaks like great dark birds.

I took the steering oar myself, and though the blade

Bit into the toppling crests, I could not force

That sinking hull's head windward—it skewed broadside

And the sea smashed and smashed and spilled sickeningly

Over the rail, in seconds so eerily bright,

Even the smallest droplets of spray hung glistening

In the shapeless flame of the storm. And one by one

The men I loved were loosed, ripped overboard

Along with the rigging or splinter of wood they clung to—

But in the roar of wind and wave, the men—
Though open-mouthed, until their hands at last
Let go—the men slipped so quietly into the swells,
As quietly as yellow leaves spin down to light
On the limpid sky of a calm stream's surface, as quietly
As a dark river winds through its silted valley,
Through its richly-figured, labyrinthine end, to the sea.

THE STORY

An enormous island of dust in the south salt air
Rises like a shadowy, veined mountain
Above the white-violet city shoals,

And roofs slant up from the undergloom of dawn:
Be still. Through watery panes, through arcs of branches,
The dark gold light of catalpa strews our street. . . .

No one's about – the town's still dead –
And the creek has fallen too low to hear: *hold still.*
Now the morning stars unsheathe in their cumulus gate. . . .

At this hour, in the story, Aeneas's sword
Flashed quick as a thought through the great, slack hawsers;
His swanlike ships slid free of the harbor sand. . . .

Then the labored breaths of the oarsmen over the bay –
A tune drifting faintly through the arras of sleep,
Until sails caught the midwinter wind. So Anna's cries

Couldn't reach them, when she found her sister dying.
But how could they know what it meant? – the waterfront
Alive with the flames of Dido's altar-pyre? –

Like a scaly brilliance woven through their wake,
Like petals lighting the deeps they longed for –
Lighting the face of the sea.

This
Water

THE DREAM

This water, falling in a sheer, blinding column
    Straight down at first, before flinging left
Over a rock shelf, narrowing in mid-air

    As if it could turn to pure sound, then funneling right
In a final leap through smoke-black spruce, absorbed
    Into the foaming green pool, is borne

On its own smooth-muscled back beneath the ledge
    Of slate, broken and sharp as ice, where I stand.
And just as the sun slips over the farthest range

    As into a towering sea, and the falls roar louder,
Pouring a season of whiteness into the deep
    Granite shade, an old dream spilling fresh

In the blood, so cold, so clear — I won't move,
    Even then. Still, the thought remains: to follow
This river through its fog-dimmed plain, through swamps

    Where the current darkens and calms, pulling
A cool, mothy robe close over its twilit
    Grassy banks. . . . So evening comes, the town

Burning through the sleep of the farms, and the farm lights
    Mark, from here, the blue dark curve of the earth —
Small fires, phantasmal starshine in ditchwater.

UNDERWAY

When the ship's bell rang, we threw down the lines,
And I waited on main deck watching the ledges
Of stucco houses, gray marble churches,
And black umbrellas collect themselves on the shore

Beneath a drizzling sky. The great six-bladed screw
Shuddered into its story, and no one spoke,
Not the men playing cards in the hard yellow light of the hold,
Nor the bridge watch staring over the high flared bow,

Nor I, charting each hour's speed in the heat
And roar of the engine-room, hand on throttle.

                    *

When we steamed from that August harbor, the evening's greens
And coppers were gathering in sheets across the Tyrrhene,
And I stood smoking out on a wing deck, resting
For the midnight watch to come. All the ship's rigging

Gleamed in the clear weather, and a pair of gulls
Came trailing us low, searching the wake. . . .
And when the sun set, toward Sicily, the smooth icy waves
Lit with a deep crimson – a welling of afterlight rising

As sun angled through stained glass changes hue –
And we crossed that light towing a mile-wide wake,

As though anchored fast in a great river's mouth. . . .
As the foaming current swept past, I imagined you

Standing out on a drenched prow of rock,
Steadfast, plowing the spuming ground swells. . . .

*

When the ship's bell rang, we eased steam to the turbines,
Backed from our slip, past the long white jetty,
And made for the straits, for the whitecapped sea.
And from the narrow perch of the fo'c'sle, I could see the fogs of
     winter

Settling in over the moored fishing boats;
And over the silent bay, the walled city quarters,
The coast with its storied ports; and over the vineyards
Weathering an iron frost, to the Alps.

And after the peninsula's seacliffs slowly collapsed
In raw billows of mist, the snow
Fell as night fell, the moon sank in its birth
To a pale light bloomed through the snow's veil.

And the sea itself disappeared; we steamed on
Leaving an empty cavern of air behind,
And my only faith then was in the engine itself,
For the stack high above kept floating down

Its own certain voice – and from below the waterline,
Through all the bulkheads and decks, rose
That sonorous hum. It was all I could hear,
All I could feel, as I glided on through the ghostly glow

Of the storm, as if the power and will to fly
Through a cold sky were in my knees and rising.

THE BRIDGE

The creek was wide, the color of lemon peel,
Or seems so now — walking there, its banks
Held me, in moldering oak leaves, shoots coming through,
Clumps of spring willow, poplar sloughing its bark,
As the marshes were held in the palm of the limestone bluffs. . . .

It was a heavy, cloudless sky, the sun burning
Above the boughs, above the still frogs among reeds
At water's edge. I was seized and drawn toward shallow
Pockets of cool shade; a curled gold leaf
Floated on in the languoring current, slowly turning. . . .

And I followed it. Spiderwebs like a warm breath
Crossed my face, and bars of sunlight broke
Apart in the motion of pushing aside a branch
To step out onto a gravel bar. There, ahead,
Was a low bridge: gray splintered oak, red iron,

Sway-backed and mossy beneath, one guard rail
Down, it nearly touched the water. With care,
I crept to its creaking middle. There, dazed with heat,
I stooped before a jagged hole, saw my head
In light, on the black water, as in a well.

Then a light rush of wind shivered the surface
Like a frieze of silver breaking —
                              and I fell back,

Eyes open to sun, head lighting on a crossbeam
So rotten, grass grew there. That image, though – like a ring
Dropped into clouding water – sank beyond dream.

This happened when I was a boy, on Cedar Creek,
And I hadn't thought of it since. But finally, today,
When the dawn haze rising off the lake
Edged over the blaze of sun on the mountainside's lace
Of snow, I looked, and didn't look back.

THE RIVER

for Larry Levis

"In a word, as my life was a life of sorrow
one way, so it was a life of mercy another. . . . "
ROBINSON CRUSOE

As she turned her face toward the afternoon light
Brimming through the half-drawn window blind —
Her beauty a kind of raft for us then —
I noticed, as if for the first time, a thin white scar
Curving from eyebrow toward her temple, and thought
In passing: if I could leave a scar like that,
Like a small burst vessel deep in the mind,
Or a phrase — or dialect — fierce, moored fast
Against ascension to longing, its telling, the light
Kindling the stacked, water-spotted glasses behind the bar. . . .

Soon the street lay sunken in a risen dusk —
All but one high storefront window, caught viridescent. . . .
And it was still enough, over the faint crack of the melting ice,
Over the soft rhythmic swell and flutter of the striped awning,
I could believe I heard the tracks two blocks away
Whisper the coal trains heaving up out of those hills . . .
And the bar hunched farther still into its corner of the hotel;
Which, though older than any of *us*, still sailed its sun-bleached
    nine floors into the full of the plains wind.
But who even slept there then? — for the veterans, still pale
From their wards, merely retired, at bar's closing, to the mezzanine,
Where they would listen simply, as in a nightlong trance,

To the solitary black whore's heels crossing the marble lobby;
And the strangers, and the sullen gray-eyed girl at the end of the bar
And I would sit wordless, watching nothing—the lucent evening
      wafting, southerly, from beyond the corner—
And gloried in it, drinking steady, as though hell itself
Were slowly dissolving, drawn toward the early constellations—
Drawn and dissolved to a deep luster we'd turn from—
A yellow light, that, for all we knew, was the season's last,

Since *all* our dreams were washed, that year, down the smoky blue
                streets,
Swirling in wave on glittering wave of sheeting rain,
Swelling the leaf-choked white limestone creekbeds,
Spilling through fragrant orchards, and gullied pastures,
And beginning the long seepage through the black floodplain,
Through the immense net of treeroots steeped
In cold alluvial night, to the Missouri.

And if we waited for the old hotel to rise and float off
      into the upper stillnesses,
If its brick façade lifted lightly as the neighborhood hawthorn lifts,
In a glimpse of moon, unclenching its limbs for the wrens of daylight;
And if we waited for all that town to rise and drift as it would,
Like a long-held breath, like a drowsy scent in the tidal dark,
We couldn't have been more patient.
                              When I knew I was dying,
Summer was rolling over my hills like the dust
From the river road, raising foliage-shaped clouds,

And painting the oak and water-elm groves at field's edge white —
Or so it looked from the river, one July day.
I was letting a friend's canoe drift broadside now and again
In rippling shallows, between mud shoals and the riverbank's
        gray tangle of driftwood. . . .
And from Rocheport down past Providence I paddled toward
        any floating thing:
A fragment of an old pier. A snag's steady wake.
A sudden mysterious thrashing behind a sandbar;
The soughing of a sycamore bent down, dragging
        its leaves in the current. . . .

And then came a low clearing: a line was strung between two oaks
Sagging with dozens of huge and glistening channel cat,
And wreathes of cabin smoke rose from somewhere,
Flattening over the mile-wide damasked river,
And I struck for the other side.
                        I pulled through the noonday heat,
Past a jutting, broken-up dike, with gray froth piled in front of it;
In its lee was a clear backwater pool, banked with cattails and rushes.

                And, rounding a willow towhead,
Where the boat kept softly nudging and scraping the silt bottom,
Where an eddy carried me circling slowly one way, then the other,
Where a nearly whole and still-green birch tree broke surface
        just beside me, and then silently sank again at once —
There, out of a sharp *kraak kraak* and slapping of air,
A great blue launched from stick nest, neck folded back,

Turned like a shield in the sun before me, streaked white breast
      as if still one moment,
And then she flattened and winged downriver, her lithe shadow
      trailing quick, cast and *gone*.

And all this time, over the wind, a steady scent of floodpools
            drying. . . .

When I headed back for the Rocheport bridge, driving hard
Upstream, a small wake sang fitfully off that hull, and I kept crossing
And crossing back, looking for slacker water.
And once, the channel caught and swung the bow
Quick as a horse swings its head in a cloud of flies.
And once, the channel broke white and churning, as if
The river were finally slipping its mask, its voice rising
As wind, after a long stillness, flares through the shadowy cornfields,
Shaking the weight of the season from out of the dusky leaves,
Rolling in great, muscled waves away toward the feathery
            treeline. . . .
But then that rapid swept on downstream, as any echoing midsummer
            storm
Lies down in the flood-carved, hawk-haunted cliffs.
And, stroke by stroke, I found a rhythm and held it;
If I paused to clear the sweat from my eyes with the back
      of a bent wrist, I lost twenty yards,
And then got it back at a leaden, dream-slow pace. . . .

So close to the shore, I could have reached out and touched
    the blue, river-smooth stones;
I could have stepped into dark summer woods, into hills
    dissolving in haze. . . .
Or in a diaphanous, golden swarm, its
Steady and measured stride consuming as it covered
One tilled field after another, and then faintly,
Into the river lull, into the damp and dead calm air
Came wafting the flat and incessant monotone of the
    grasshoppers. . . .

But then that too was pierced by an airhorn's volleying shriek,
As a coal barge centered in the upstream bend, wheeling
Toward me into its marks, and toward me rolled
Its crashing and river-wide bow wave. The tug followed, shimmering
In its heat, with black smoke blown straight out from its stack,
And the horn booming down again, but louder.

So why did I keep laboring on upriver, leaving swirling circles
    in the woven surface behind me? — as though
If I pushed hard enough through the heat and the heat's chimeras,
Delicately tracing the eddy between channel and bank,
Beneath sun-flooded elms, then I might disappear. . . .

Now I could hear the harsh moan of the diesels swelling,
And that small, silken mountain of coal loomed like a gray-blue
    cloud, closer;
It was then I plunged the oar-blade into the deep

And turned on that aching arch of muscle – the ropes through my
        arms and back;
With the riverboat's horn-blast washing the banks, the barge's rust-
        streaked
   prow square at my back;

With the channel now wave-crossed and crowded, jostling me toward
        the rocks
   of shore, shoving me back;
With a freshening wind off a thousand miles of river
Smelling of North Platte clay and the violence of prairie
   gathering huge at my back:
It was *then* I turned, and taken then, I blent headlong
   with the power of that god,
And fell through the heart of my country.

THE HAVEN

Lightly as falling, I slipped bodiless
Through gaps in the branches, through stand after stand
Of cedars shouldering each other close
On the low blond hills or sinkhole slopes, and wound up winded
Near a sunken, snowmelt stream;
Along its banks, the frozen grass lay folded
In waves, and still hid patches of snow. A drumming
Of wings passed overhead, and I shivered, swept
With a memory of you as you woke.
The creek itself was a dark stair of pools linked

By a small, clear-spun strand in the crystalline
Bird-tracked silt. Though I felt no wind, a murmuring ran
Through the bark, all around, of the sycamore trunks —
More shadow than substance — staring out
Through the milky air. *You were rising*
In a distant hour, wrapped in a warmth
Of sunlight. And then I was back in it, as
The dull bronze haze of daybreak loomed
Over the farthest ridge, and from the town
Beyond, the slurred speech of traffic rose to the ear.

FISH CREEK FALLS

The town spreads clear and still in the late June wind,
Violet as river water at day's end,
And another strand of tail lights floats apart
On the mountain pass, spanning the houseless dark.

Now stars come on, on the fine-haired crest of the mountains;
Now a trailing cloudbank fires in the blaze
Drawn flickering low through the aspen. Now a glaze
On the sharp blue tin roof where we slept. . . .
                                        It stands
Summer-surrounded now, like the falls in their fold,
In their full, white, still-sculpted roar, in that cold
And resiny air. Just once, then, everything plain:

A dragonfly hung near, and a small trout arced
Clear of the spray, which kept rising halfway
Toward the fall's lip, only to fall again.

ELEGY FOR TOM MCAFEE

(1 9 2 8 - 1 9 8 2)

Like an old unburnished fiction, this one began
Abruptly, a hundred ways at once, my mind
Beside itself and looking for the lost
Traces of a real night outside,
With the sounds of the dark islanded masses of trees
On the hills beyond, as if voices were in them:

And began as sudden as bats when they pour like smoke
From a cave or bridge-arch, their shivering cries
Like a hoard of thoughts, a plain song trailed off over
The green and ochre lights of the river. . . .
Near the landing where I stood,
There were hidden boats knocking softly side to side,
And figures were drifting weightless through the fog,
They would briefly form and then disappear in the folds
Of luminous darkness, their muffled words
Off-pitched and slurred, though I wanted to hear them, wanted
To see them more than anything. A truck
That roared overhead sent waves of shock
Through the pilings, shearing the moonless calm
Like cloth. . . . I was trying to lift my numb, slowed feet,
And the ceiling was slanted with white April sun,
Its bleak light catching on every edge. Of course,
This was only a dream. But it did begin like this.

Movies were all I could stand — the engulfing sadness? —
Above the pointless and false balustrades,
Dim chandeliers dripped amber glass down into

The floodlit and even falser dusk. The crowd
Was anonymously settled in the colossal lake
Of silence, and in that sense that the house lights
Have already started to wane. And after a minute,
The curtain *would* come open, the screen glowing
Blue as a sulphurous fire. I knew you were there,
One night, before I saw you — *thought* I saw you
Off in the wings, sitting straight up in your scarf,
The splay of light drifting over your reading glasses.
I wouldn't look again, but I heard your laugh
Ring clearly, once. *Yours.*

                 It was an endless fall:
The sky filed past its low identical whorls
Of opaque white, the sun was all but forgotten,
And even the façades of the Broadway shops
All sank away within themselves, and downtown
Closed like a fist. Leaving the bar at closing,
Full of bourbon and smoke, I'd stand, sometimes,
In the shadows of the bank:
                   I won't forget
The ashy lights of that town in the dark silk air.
I gulped the wind that whipped my coat behind me,
And almost walked right into you where you stood
In the sepia that fused one thing to another. *Is it you?*
I said. . . . In the awful silence, I touched your sleeve;
The warp of night went sifting through my fingers.

Then the last exhalations of warmth rose from the sidewalks,
And in the fields beyond, the long yellow grass
Poked through the snow as it always had, bowed from the last
Hard weather, arced beneath the shadows of clouds
As if it were still alive. . . . But I didn't see it.
The hills were like iron, and my life had come to nothing.

I was catching my breath at the top of the stair. I looked
Back where you waited there in the downward halflight,
Nearly as one with the silvering glass of the door,
Just touching the rail in your own tranquil way,
That merest hesitation. And I suddenly knew
You had come to face my wild and helpless anger
At your death. We stood like that, it seemed, forever,
But I turned from you with everything left to say.

                    *

I seldom dream these days, and think of you less and less.
Our housefront rides the same oceanic spill
Of hours, and the dark arms of the locust hide
A perfectly motionless, perfectly lucid evening.
In the smell of a chicken baking, with work on the table,
There is no world beneath. Nor can shadows
Come from there;
                    but still, from the interstices,
From the crooked rooflines and ghostly undersides
Of the sycamore's giant leaves, what comes

Comes unforeseen, unguessed at, into the rifts
Of an August twilight, loosed in the piercing
Lust of cicadas and swallows, the slow dreamsongs:

A block down the street in your suburb, a man is standing
Up to his waist in shade, his face gold-lit,
His hand strangely raised. You are alone,
Completely adrift in that shade yourself, and your street
Lies changed, waist-deep in a hush of coolness turning
Mirror-dark, enveloping everyone's lawn,
As the houses light one molten room at a time,
And the faint white, arrowy limbs of the streetlights reach
Through every city quarter, a webwork glimmering
Along the floor of the great shadow pool,
                                        for this
Is the hour the dark verge rises, reclaiming more
Than the front range of foothills, like so many coins:
There go the aster, and fields of lupine; there go
The mined-out canyons, and delicate talus slopes;
There goes the silhouetted Wasatch crest,
Like a giant asleep at the blood light's edge —
And gone are its lightning burns and its summer snows,
Its handful of stars, its wordless wind, and its sky.

LINES FOR FALL

Why is it we always imagine an empty station
With a newspage blown across it, with a waiting figure
Bundled against the early hour? Trees vein
The summer darkness, where finally, the indistinct

Low breathings of the train come drifting on
The air like a pattern of the heart. Or we think
Of a girl alone on a runway, hair and dress
Rippling with light—such are the terms of absence.

But you know it as well as I do when it comes:
Books slip from the hand as if nothing were in them.
Someone's music seeps through the walls. Sunsets
Flame in the windows like rows of maples. . . .

THE SOLVING MEMORY OF THINGS

Regardless how nonchalantly you walk
Through the flickering delicate interlock of shade,
You can never quite approach whatever it is
That disappears at the peripheries of leaves
And light – a memory like a bird slipped free
And flitting ahead as it might have done in life –
Across the concave of a phantom riverbed
Sunk in the trees, where the deep diluvial chill
Of March is strongest. And something tells you
You won't catch sight of it again by looking
Directly for it. . . .
              The branches on all sides
Grow eerily, impenetrably thick here,
So already you wonder what the idea was,
What inland-tidal pull, from long back, rose
Against the nature of your present self,
And plunked you down in a whorl of raveled limbs?

(Stuck in an unnoticed corner of sky, forgotten,
Blotted by clouds, hangs the gray, flat disc of the sun.)

And where is the path you would follow (nervously jangling
The keys and change in your pocket) if the woods
It wove through are half washed away in flood
Each spring? And how will you ever find your way out,
With all sense of direction vanished; the passing of time
So strangely numbed; and the images you remembered
Turning to air as you grope through bloodroot and cobweb? –

Down the wrong roads of insomnia, into
The sycamores, the nightmare trees:
                                        and beyond
Their caverned silence lies a heartbreaking vastness
Of wind-muscled fields; and then open marshes,
Looms of sumac where mosquitoes rise
Like heat through the swampy and heron-haunted air:

For *there* is the empire of nostalgia, a smokefall
Of dusk lain over the riffling pewter skin
Of the river. And *there* is the lace-iron bridge,
The banks of driftwood and tires and rusted cans
Of adolescence, that echoing broken land.

So you find yourself looking up, far above, at the lapis
Gaps in the canopy, watching the clouds pass over
And over again in the northward current of sky;
And you think: *they are not of us*, those dramas of mansions
Falling in, catastrophes of towers
And terraces. . . .
                    And they are not written words,
Nor the drift of seraphic dreams, but water from over
The mountains, evolving its instants of dissolution. . . .

Until finally, even down here, there is something alive
Far back in the cottonwoods, trapped in the densest meshes,

\ Straining its great clawed limbs down the long aisles
Of pillared shade:

                and this, too, is the sun.

And the rounded, primordial outlines of limestone cliffs
Invent themselves, in a new hard brightness of air;
And the ivy's dark green river of hands splashes over
The foot of them; as the sound of water faintly
Unlocks, in the mossy springs that drip down the cliffsides,
Commencing their implausibly intricate cursive
Through the dark distillations of woods. . . .

                          And, in the motion of a
      moment,
Against an almost unconscious backcloth of grapevines
Let down out of the treetops;

                  and in the slow burn
Of the muted and ghostly violets washing surflike
Around your ankles, covering what softly breaks
Beneath your weight,

             you take another step.

A U T H O R ' S   N O T E

Michael White was born in 1956. He is a graduate
of the University of Missouri and the University of
Utah (Ph.D. 1990), and has taught creative writing
at the University of Missouri, the University of
Utah, and Westminster College in Fulton, Missouri.
Among many other awards, he won the Academy of
American Poets Prize three times at Utah. He was
married to Jackie White, a professor of Theatre at
the University of Texas at Austin, who died of can-
cer in 1991.

The type in this book is Bodoni.

Composition by the Typeworks.

Cover by Theodore van Rysselberghe,

"Big Clouds," 1893,

© Indianapolis Museum of Art,

The Holliday Collection.